—Jennifer

BECAUSE I SAID SO!

Continue to be

an amazing

mother.

BECAUSE I SAID SO!
Published by Purposely Created Publishing Group™
Copyright © 2017 Leona Carter

Printed in the United States of America
ISBN: 978-1-945558-76-4

Special discounts are available on bulk quantity purchases by book clubs, associations and special interest groups. For details email:
sales@publishyourgift.com
or call (888) 949-6228.

For information logon to:
www.PublishYourGift.com

BECAUSE I SAID SO!

EQUIPPING AND INSPIRING MOTHERS TO BE INTENTIONAL ABOUT THE WORDS THEY SPEAK

Leona Carter

DEDICATION

This book is dedicated to my husband, Omarr, and our six children, the Carter Crew. Thank you, Omarr, for your unwavering commitment to our family. I am blessed to be a part of such a magnificent tribe.

TABLE OF CONTENTS

Dedication v

Preface 1

Chapter 1: Don't Say Nothin' At All 3

Chapter 2: Easter Sunday 7

Chapter 3: One and Three 11

Chapter 4: Nine Months 15

Chapter 5: 100-Mile Radius 19

Chapter 6: Back Pay 23

Chapter 7: Our Little Michigander 29

Chapter 8: Yes You Can 33

Chapter 9: Come In 37

Chapter 10: Intentional 41

Chapter 11: Imagine 49

About the Author 55

PREFACE

I was compelled to write this book because I wanted to share my experience and knowledge as a mother. Many have asked how two high school sweethearts came through such a tremendous life journey that resulted in the Carter Crew. As you read this book, you will see that, by being intentional about the words we spoke, our family encountered many remarkable life situations.

The purpose of this book is to equip and inspire mothers to be intentional about their words. Everything you say matters and can be held against you. But the good news is that you have the authority to change anything you don't like. With that being said, this book outlines how you can become clear about what you hope to obtain in life. The stories in this book are all real episodes from my life, my reality, and they occurred thanks to the words I spoke intentionally. This journey started in high school and, for the past twenty years, the reality of my intentionality has developed into more than I could've ever hoped for.

I appreciate my family who was instrumental in the writing of my book. When I had questions or needed to get input, the Carter Crew willingly helped, and I also got to share a lot with my children about how our family came to be as strong as we are—it was a great experience. I am grateful to God for allowing so many wonderful things to happen to us in this lifetime. Many of my experiences truly are once-in-a-lifetime.

CHAPTER 1

DON'T SAY NOTHIN' AT ALL

"Believe you can and you're halfway there."
—Theodore Roosevelt

"Don't say that!" My mom said.

I rebutted, "What's the big deal? I didn't mean anything by it."

When I was a girl growing up in Seattle, Washington, my family was always conscious of what they said. As a kid, you too might have felt the way I did: You say how you feel with no prior thought to the words spoken. I didn't know the reason *why* I couldn't say "bad things" other than because my mom said so.

I grew up in a large family. My mother was my dad's second marriage, so my five older siblings were already grown and on their own, and the remaining five children were at home. As a family, we attended church often and placed great emphasis on always being on our best behavior and having proper manners, especially when talking to adults—the time-old "respect your elders." Of my siblings, I was child number six. This meant that I had older siblings telling me what to do and I had the pleasure of telling my younger siblings what to do. I grew up learning how to be both a leader and a follower, even though my younger siblings would probably be inclined to call what I had "bossy-ship" skills.

I would often get into run-ins and fall-outs with my four younger brothers. One day, when running around the house, furious at one of my little brothers for taking my piggy bank, I yelled, "I'm gonna kill you!" Immediately, everything stopped. All was quiet and you could hear a pin drop in the stillness. I slowly and hesitantly turned to my mother. The look on her face immediately told me something was wrong. She confirmed my suspicion and I was the one who got in trouble. Yelling the words, "I'm gonna kill you" outweighed my brother's taking my piggy bank—in my mother's eyes, there was no comparison. I clearly lost that battle because of saying something so harmful with my words.

Words impacted my family dynamics strongly. I could pop one of my brothers on the back of the head and not get in as much trouble as I would if I said something detrimental to him. You could not and still cannot say "those kinds of things" in our house. We were reminded time and time again, if you don't have something nice to say, don't say anything at all, or as my mother would say, "Don't say nothin' at all." As a kid, I didn't really get the big picture but I learned quickly just how powerful my words are.

When I was sixteen-years-old, I desired to know my purpose on a deeper level. As a young teen, I attended church services with my family and began to understand that there was more to be learned and felt than what I was experiencing during our spiritual services together. On the cusp between 1992 and 1993, I went to a church service on New Year's Eve with my family. We arrived at ten pm on December 31st, and as we did every year, we began to pray the old year out and pray the new year in. We would not leave until after the clock struck midnight.

As a tenth grader, I never experienced having a boy-friend in high school because I felt that I didn't have time for one. I had planned out college and I didn't have time to waste on a boy. But during that prayer time at church, I suddenly was taken by a desire to meet my husband. It was strange to me because I can honestly tell you that this desire was *never* there before. Even still, I prayed out loud to God that night: "If I am going to be married, then I am ready to meet my husband now."

Seventeen days later, I started dating, Omarr, who is now my husband of twenty-one years. To this day, we remember that we started dating January 17, 1993, and our friends laugh at how we can remember it so clearly. We know because I spoke those powerful words twenty-three years ago. We now acknowledge January 17th as our Date-O-versary. This answered prayer was a launch into a deeper understanding: Because I said so, it was so!

CHAPTER 2

EASTER SUNDAY

*"Nothing is impossible; the word itself
says 'I'm possible.'"*
—**Audrey Hepburn**

In 1995, Omarr and I graduated from Foster High School in Tukwila, Washington. Right after high school, he joined the United States Marine Corp and went directly to boot camp at the Marine Corp Recruit Depot in San Diego, California. While home planning the wedding, I was wrought by the excitement and tension of having everything done in time. Three months later, when Omarr had returned home after completing boot camp, we married the next day. Three months out of high school, here we were: High school sweethearts, starting our new life together as husband and wife. We went away on our honeymoon to Ocean Shores, Washington, where we spent ten blissful days in the sun as newlyweds. Upon returning home to Seattle, Omarr left the next day for his new station at Camp Pendleton, California. I stayed in Seattle, and we visited each other once a month until housing was available. After six months, I was able to join my husband in Oceanside, California.

The summer of 1996, I learned that I was pregnant with our first child and we were very excited. I remember going to an appointment for the Women, Infants, and Children (WIC), a special supplemental nutrition program for these groups that provide federal grants to states for supplemental foods, health care referrals, and nutrition education for pregnant, breastfeeding, and non-breastfeeding postpartum women, and to infants and children up to age five who are found to be at nutritional risk.

While waiting in the lobby to meet with the nutritionist, there were many mothers with children running around in the crowded room. I observed a mother talking rudely to her toddler child. She cursed and fussed at the child so loudly, telling them to shut up and sit down. As a new expectant mother, just shy of three months pregnant, I stared in disbelief and looked around to see if anyone else was paying attention at how mean this mother was talking to her child, but nobody took note. It just seemed normal in that atmosphere.

While sitting there, I thought to myself, how could a mother talk to her child that way? My mother had never treated me in that manner when I was growing up. I had not experienced motherhood yet, but I already knew that I would never talk to my child that way. As mothers, it doesn't matter how old your child is—we have to be intentional about the words we say to and around our children.

Now don't get me wrong: Twenty years later, I've said some things to my children that I wish I could change, but as a standard, I have always chosen to speak life. We have to be conscious that we are shaping their thoughts, behaviors, and habits with our words. Imagine the trajectory of a child's life when all they have heard growing up are how horrible they are, how they can't do anything right, all with cursing and demeaning phrases. Imagine what a mother does for their child's future when she talks in that demeaning way.

That day, I vowed never to degrade, belittle, or curse at my children and that I would always do my very best to speak life and light to my children.

At the doctor's appointment, I was told that my due date was March 11, 1997. But as soon as Omarr learned of the date, he announced, "My first child will be born on my birthday," which was March 31st. He held onto that declaration for nine months. Then, on Easter Sunday, March 30th, after being two weeks overdue, I went into labor at church and had to be rushed to the hospital. After thirteen long hours, I gave birth to a healthy baby girl on March 31st at 1:32 am. She was my husband's twenty-first birthday present. The atmosphere was charged with the words Omarr spoke for the entire nine-month pregnancy, and he got what he wanted.

His first child was born on his birthday because he said so!

CHAPTER 3

ONE AND THREE

*"Whether you think you can, or you think
you can't—you're right."*

—Henry Ford

We always knew we wanted a big family. Omarr was an
only child in his household (he had a younger sister in
a different state) and, in my household, I had siblings
coming out the seams. While in Oceanside, we had another daughter in 1998 and Omarr finished his military
assignment after being honorably discharged from the
Marine Corps. We moved back to Seattle in July 1999.
As blessed as I was to be able to bear children, I did not
weather pregnancy well. In May of 2000, we had another
daughter and during this pregnancy, I was put on be-
drest for three months before I delivered. I knew that
would be my last pregnancy. Omarr and I agreed that, if
we wanted any more children, we would adopt.

In 2002, after our youngest daughter turned two, we were ready to start our journey towards adoption because, believe it or not, we had a little more room in our quiver. During my high school years, I often admired when close friends of mine adopted children into their homes and they became part of the family. I observed how the new additions blended so well within the family and I knew I wanted to do so one day. I even asked Omarr, who was my boyfriend at the time, if he would ever adopt children. "I wouldn't mind," he said. "But I would get married first and start our family. Then, from there, we will see." Well, that's what we did.

Months later after finishing up all the required training classes, a caseworker came over to do an assessment and intake. Sitting across the table with a pen and paper, she asked my husband and me, "Have you thought about what type of child you would like to adopt?" My husband and I looked at each other and I smiled because I knew exactly what I wanted.

I stated to the caseworker, "As a matter of fact, yes, I have. I would like to adopt two African American boys. I want the boys to be biological brothers. I want the younger brother to be a one-year-old and the older brother to be three-years-old. Because we have three daughters, I want to ensure that they do not have a history of sexual abuse or destructive behavior."

The caseworker looked at us with a surprised grin on her face. She chuckled a little bit and said, "Wow, you do know what you want, huh?" As the meeting came to a close, we walked the her to the door and she informed us that, as soon as she heard anything, she would let us know.

Approximately ten days later, our caseworker called us to see if we were available to meet two little boys. I began to ask questions on the phone: How old the boys were? One and three years old. Were they brothers? Yes. When were their birthdays? I could hear the caseworker fumble through her papers, and after a moment of quiet, she answered that the older one's birthday was December 3rd and the younger boy's birthday was May 9th, I stopped in my tracks: My youngest daughter's birthday was May 9, 2000. Thinking I needed to clean the wax out of my ears, I asked her to repeat what she said. She confirmed, "Yes, May 9, 2002." Not only were the boys one and three years old as I desired, but one of the boys shared a birthday with my youngest daughter. We set a time to meet the boys that evening, and as soon as I saw them, I knew they were our sons. We adopted and went from three children to five.

CHAPTER 4

NINE MONTHS

*"Don't use your words to describe the situation.
Use your words to change the situation."*
—Joel Osteen

The summer of 2005, Omarr and I felt that it was time for a change. Our family was thriving, our jobs were consistent, and nothing was wrong, but we believed the near future was going to look different than planned. We didn't know what that meant or what kind of change was coming, but it felt immense. My husband sensed the change involved being out of state. The only place we had lived outside of our hometown of Seattle was Oceanside, where my husband served four years in the Marine Corps. Because of the uncertainty of what our next steps were, Omarr and I agreed to start a nine-month prayer to get clarity and direction for our next big "change" that we knew nothing about.

We started the prayer in September of that same year. We got up every Sunday morning at 4 am, dressed all five kids, and drove to our church to start prayer by 5 am, which went on until 8 am. This was a family prayer, not a church-led event; so, we ensured our prayer time did not conflict with our regular church services, which started at 9:30 am. Once prayer ended at 8 am, we had an hour and a half to freshen up, get breakfast for the kids, which we brought with us, and get ready for our regular Sunday morning service. Occasionally, our pastor, M. L. Tucker, arrived a little earlier to pray with us towards the end of our prayer session. We did this every Sunday for nine months (which was a total of forty days) until June 2006.

Three weeks into our nine-month prayer, I received heart-wrenching news that two of my younger brothers were arrested for first-degree murder. When I heard the news, I was in disbelief, thinking it was a possible case of mistaken identity. I knew my brothers did not lead a life of crime, drugs, or anything close to it: One of my brothers just graduated with his bachelors of arts in business sports management and my other brother was three credits away from his degree in psychology—they *must* have gotten the wrong people.

I called both of my brothers and got no answer, just busy signals on both phones. I went down the list, calling siblings and my parents. Everyone was stunned at the news and didn't know anything more than I did, but we were instructed by one of my older brothers to watch the ten o'clock news. I had three more hours to go but I wasn't waiting until ten o'clock so I parked right in front of the television for the next four hours with endless tears flowing down my face. During commercials, there was news preview for what would be aired at ten and there they were: In the seven-second preview were my two brothers in a bright orange jumpsuit with handcuffs on their wrists and chains around their ankles. I sat there staring at the TV in utter disbelief, anxiety, and fear with another round of tears staining my face.

When the program did finally air, all I could do was hold my hands over my mouth as I listened to the news anchor unfold the shocking details of why I would not be able to hug my brothers anytime soon: They were involved in an altercation outside of an apartment complex of a nineteen-year-old college football player, who was ultimately shot and killed. Both brothers were arrested and due for sentencing in the coming weeks.

That night I slept on my living room floor in front of the TV, where I felt closest to my brothers. Dazed, I slept on my pillow of tears until it was morning.

CHAPTER 5

100-MILE RADIUS

"Live life to the fullest, and focus on the positive."
—Matt Cameron

As time passed, we learned more details about my brothers' incident: The two had driven to meet the football player to ask him questions about a fight that had broke out the night before at a nightclub, which involved another brother of mine and a cousin. Things got out of hand during the conversation, two shots were fired at the young man, who later died at the hospital. Both brothers pleaded guilty to a lesser degree of second-degree murder.

Omarr and I continued our Sunday morning prayer sessions and, needless to say, I surely had some things to pray about, even if it was just a tear-shedding session. I asked God many questions, mostly why and how something so horrible could be happening to our family.

Two months later, there was a court hearing where I testified as a character witness for my two brothers. The court hearing was in Moscow, Idaho, and my mom, my friend Ta'vin, and I drove eight hours from Seattle to stay with my best friend, Evonne, who was attending college nearby. We left early Wednesday morning and arrived in Idaho that evening and made preparations for court the next morning.

When I approached the witness stand, I testified about how my brothers were both true gentlemen and upstanding characters. Due to the high-profile nature of the case, the courtroom was packed like sardines with family, friends, and every TV camera and news reporter within a 100-mile radius. For what seemed like forever, cameras flashed, people sobbed, lawyers chatted, and all of them together sounded like blurring fog horns in the distant.

When all was said and done, the judge rendered his verdict and my two brothers were deemed to serve the next decade of their young life behind bars. Stunned beyond what I could feel, I watched my brothers leave the courtroom. I was only able to wave from a distance. I briefly talked to other family members, trying to appear stronger than I actually was, and quickly made my departure. We returned back to Evonne's house to unpack all the emotions we were feeling after coming to terms with the fact that my brothers were not coming home with us.

Later that evening, Ta'vin alerted me to the news channel where community leaders from Kalamazoo, Michigan were unveiling a new program called The Kalamazoo Promise. Still, in a slight fog, I didn't think much of it because my thoughts and emotions were still entangled with my brothers. All I could do was pack our things for the next day's trip.

Upon arriving home, I shared information with my husband and the kids, who stayed in Seattle. Without getting too emotional or sharing too many details, I told the kids, who were all under the age of ten, that their uncles would be okay. All they knew was that their uncles got in trouble and mom was sad about it.

Approximately two weeks later during our Sunday morning prayer, I felt a strong impression or feeling in my heart that the opportunity or "change" that we sensed had something to do with the information Ta'vin shared about The Kalamazoo Promise. I recalled our conversation and the details she shared. I remember her saying,

"You have five kids and this would be a good opportunity to send them to college." All the light bulbs went off in my head and a big a-ha moment was evident. Before sharing any information with my husband, I began to research Kalamazoo and learn all about The Kalamazoo Promise.

CHAPTER 6

———

BACK PAY

*"You cannot have a positive life and
a negative mind."*

—Joyce Meyer

For the next few days, I studied the press release for The Kalamazoo Promise and learned all I could about it. The Kalamazoo Promise is a four-year scholarship program for all students who reside within the boundaries of the Kalamazoo Public School (KPS). Upon graduating from a KPS high school, The Kalamazoo Promise covers tuition and mandatory fees at any college or university within the state of Michigan, including private colleges and universities. The amount of tuition covered is based on when a student enrolled in KPS. If a student started their KPS journey at kindergarten and graduated from one of the KPS high schools, their tuition would be covered at 100%. There is a sliding scale based on your entry point into KPS. The least amount a student could receive would be entering high school at ninth grade, receiving 65% of the tuition.

I knew that if we were going to take up this new opportunity, it would involve our family moving from Seattle to Kalamazoo. At the current ages of our children, we would qualify for approximately half a million dollars in scholarship for our children. With the sliding scale, our oldest child would receive 90% of the tuition program, our next two would receive 95%, and our two youngest would receive 100% of the tuition program. When I did the math for our large family, this opportunity seemed well worth the move. Now it was time to share this information with Omarr.

During dinner one evening, I told my husband that moving to Michigan would afford us the opportunity to pay for most of our children's college education. "Michigan?" Omarr said. "I don't know anything about Michigan." He quickly changed the subject. I realized that this was going to be harder than I thought.

From that point, I continued to do research on Kalamazoo. I looked at schools, churches, and houses. As time went on, I gave this move serious consideration and I would bring up the subject of moving to Michigan periodically to my husband, who would ask questions. I now had the answers. I continued to pray on Sundays that Omarr would come around to this opportunity.

After the holidays, I sat and talked with my husband seriously about what it would take to move to Kalamazoo. I told him how much it would be for moving costs and everything we would need. I told him that, with our current savings, we would need $2500 in order to successfully make the move to Michigan. At this point, I was 100% sure that this was the move our family was supposed to make but my husband was only at about 45%. I told him that I would love to move at the end of August so that our kids could start off the new school year in Michigan. He really thought that I had lost it, because I had given this so much thought down to the first day of school. He stated, "If we don't have the money by August then we won't be moving anywhere." That was understandable, so I spoke while looking up to the ceiling, hoping God could hear me, in my living room. I told Him, "I need $2500 to move by August 25th." It's a good thing we still had a few more months left in our nine-month prayer.

When June arrived and our prayer came to an end, I was now 150% sure that this was our time and we *were* moving to Michigan. Omarr was at about 51%. I slowly started packing our basement and cleaning things out, but not to the point that I had to explain to my kids what I was doing. I donated things to Goodwill and got rid of any extras that I did not want to transport. Occasionally, Omarr would give me a look as if to say, "This girl is really serious."

At the end of July, I received a letter in the mail. It read:

Dear Mrs. Carter,

We have been informed that you are now the adoptive mother of (child's name) who previously became eligible for social security benefits because of his biological father (father's name). He has been eligible since birth and enclosed is a check that is back pay for the last two years.

Enclosed is a check for $2632.

Sincerely,
Seattle Social Security Office

Can you believe it? We received this check four weeks before our departure date. I was elated at what God did for us. All I could think about was, "Wait 'til Omarr sees this!" Later, when he came home from work, I just put the check on the table before serving dinner and let him see the letter next to it. Sitting down at the dining room table, he asked, "What is this for?"

I explained, "Our two-year-old son is eligible for benefits and they paid us current and back pay. This is the money we need to move to Michigan."

Omarr's mouth dropped opened, and once I helped him close it, he said, "Whoa, whoa, that's God. Whew, whoa, that's God." He stayed stunned in his seat, while I screamed and jumped around in excitement. Whatever doubt Omarr had about moving was now erased. We had to officially make the transition by informing our jobs and families.

Later that evening, I saw Omarr packing boxes so fast, asking, "Where do you want these boxes at?" I simply laughed because prior to our blessing arriving in the mail he had not packed one box. Grateful that Omarr and I were now on the same page, it was time to share the news with our children.

CHAPTER 7

OUR LITTLE MICHIGANDER

"I believe if you keep your faith, you keep your trust, you keep the right attitude, if you're grateful, you'll see God open up new doors."
—Joel Osteen

In August 2006, we moved from Seattle, Washington to Kalamazoo, Michigan. We hired a moving company to haul our furnishings from the 206 to the 269. My husband and I drove our minivan with all five kids and made it a fun road trip, stopping in Oklahoma to see one of my best friends on the way. We arrived in Michigan on September 1, 2006, a week before school started. We spent the next week looking like tourists, ooh-ing and aw-ing at everything.

On the first day of school, we were interviewed by Channel 3 News, because of our decision to move here for The Kalamazoo Promise. I enrolled five children under the age of ten in the Kalamazoo Public Schools and became the recipient of "Five Little Promises." This was the first full school year since the announcement about The Kalamazoo Promise made national news last fall.

We stayed in apartment complexes for three months until our house sold in Seattle on November 14th. The next day, we closed on our house in Kalamazoo. We worked with an excellent realtor named Jim Hess with Jaqua Realtors, who learned of our story and, with our permission, forwarded the information to a contact at the *New York Times*. Guess what? The *Times* did a full-cover story of our decision to partake in The Kalamazoo Promise. It was awesome to see our whole family with a huge picture and article, and then to be able to share the news with my family and friends back home. It was a pretty amazing first year in Kalamazoo. It ended with our local newspaper, *The Kalamazoo Gazette*, also covering our story.

Approximately ten months after getting settled, we started the application process to adopt another child: Our little Michigander. The licensing curriculum in Michigan was the same as Washington's to foster-and-adopt; therefore, we just needed to take a refresher course. I once again had a heart-to-heart with my case worker and shared with her that I wanted to adopt a one-year-old African American little girl who did not have any history of sexual abuse or destructive behavior. I also told her that I would love to have our new addition in our home before my thirtieth birthday, which was about forty days away.

We soon received a phone call from our caseworker about our meeting a beautiful little girl. Just like last time, I asked how old she was: A one-year-old African American little girl. I asked when her birthday was: June 2006. I immediately yelled to my husband, who was in the other room, *"Her birthday is in June! Woo hoo!"*

Let me explain. By her birthday being in June of 2006, this means that she was in the womb of her birth mother during the same nine months we were in our nine-month prayer in Seattle, which ended in June 2006. Well, I was absolutely convinced that this was our little girl. She arrived in our home four days before my thirtieth birthday. I had a great birthday celebration with my husband and our six children, whom we now refer to as the Carter Crew.

In November 2015, The Kalamazoo Promise celebrated its ten-year anniversary. I was privileged to be a part of the video tribute by sharing what The Kalamazoo Promise meant for our family. To date, we are the largest Promise family since it launched in 2005. The Carter Crew now has six little promises.

CHAPTER 8

YES YOU CAN

"You are the average of the five people you spend the most time with."

—Jim Rohn

You have the power to form your world by the words that you speak. What words have you spoken to you children today? Remember when your toddlers first learned to write their names: Wrought with difficulty and frustration, they slumped back in their chairs and said, "I can't do it." You got down to eye-level and encouraged them by saying, "Yes, you can." When those powerful words met their ears, it stirred confidence inside them and gave them bold tenacity to try again, because the atmosphere was charged with, "Yes, you can." And guess what? They did.

The power of your words is a conscious choice that you make every day. Imagine this scenario: It's early morning and you are helping your child get dressed for school. You see your child appears sad and you ask them what is wrong. They state that they are nervous about a test they have to take at school today. Your child is entrusting you with their vulnerability. At this moment, you can choose words of life and encouragement or words of doom and defeat. What are you going to say to your child? As a mother, you understand that the words you say will leave a lasting memory of reassurance or detriment to your child. What will you choose? Every day, we are given small opportunities to make a big impact.

Now, In the above example, you may believe that you would definitely make the choice of encouraging your child. But now, imagine having this conversation when you are running late for a meeting, haven't eaten breakfast, and have another toddler in the other room banging on the wall from their crib. These external factors may adversely affect what would have been an easy conversation to have. As a result of the other distractions, you may come off as short-tempered, uncaring, and unhelpful, because your response to your child is, "I'm sure you will figure it out."

In this way, as mothers, we must constantly worry about whether or not we did and said the right thing. At times, if feels like we are playing trial-and-error, and often getting the latter. But the difference is in this question: Are you approaching your children with intention or are you only reacting to them? Begin by deciding what you want your children to know about life and show them the importance of their character and words.

Here is an example of one lesson I learned in my late teens and one I now teach my own children. Years before I knew anything about how to be intentional with my words or thoughts, I learned as a young girl not to say "bad things" and not to surround myself with "negativity." Did I completely understand what was bad or negative? Not always. Because my family was protective over my siblings and me, we didn't experience until our late teen years the effects of being around negative situations with our friends (or so-called friends).

One day, I came home with a negative vibe. I smart-mouthed my mother after she asked me to do chores. The first thing she said was, "Who have you been hanging around?" I thought to myself, what does that have to do with anything? But my mother continued on to tell me that my attitude had changed and whoever I was hanging around was affecting me detrimentally.

I was shocked because, sure enough, I had recently begun hanging around a few girls that I thought were cool, but would tell you off in a minute with a bad attitude. I didn't know that hanging around them would affect *my* attitude. Believe me, I learned real quick to minimize my time with these friends and to check my attitude before I got home.

Now, using my own experience, I teach the same thing to my children!

CHAPTER 9

COME IN

*"Once you replace negative thoughts with positive
ones, you'll start having positive results."*
—**Willie Nelson**

I was winding down at home one evening after a long
day at work. I mentally unpacked my day before diving
into the evening rituals of checking my kids' homework,
making sure they got in the tub, doing room checks to
confirm I can see the floor, and delegating one of the kids
to start dinner (if my husband was not home yet). Omarr
often works late nights, but he is the Carter Chef and I
only cook if I have to, which usually means he or the kids
are not home.

While in my room, I heard a knock on the door. I
gently called out, "Come in," and my teenage daughter
opened the door to make sure I hadn't forgotten about
dinner (which usually means, "Who did you tell to start

dinner or should I start it?"). I assured her that I hadn't forgotten and would be out momentarily. Approximately two minutes later, I heard another knock on the door. Not so gently as before, I replied, "Come in!" My son opened the door, telling me that he needed his permission slip signed. I pointed to the inbox, where we turn in all papers the night before that need to be signed. He put his slip in the box and moseyed on his way. Thirty seconds later, another child came knocking on the door. With all my gentleness depleted, I yelled, "*Come in!*" This time, I had a shakiness in my voice, as if trying to sing a note five octaves higher than my range. My youngest daughter wanted to show me a picture she had made at school. As I climbed down from the falsetto note I just hit, I realized my youngest daughter didn't know that she was the third consecutive knock I had received and, therefore, didn't realize that the edge I had in my voice had nothing to do with her. Each child knocked on my door, without realizing that one of his or her siblings knocked moments before.

I realized that, as a mother of six children, you have to have a system for everything, even to relax for a few minutes. I thought I would be able to quietly steal away for a few minutes to regroup for the evening activities, but they all knew where to find me and sought me out.

So, I developed a system called "Mommy break." I created a simple, clearly-written sign to post on my door stating, "MOM TIME: PLEASE DO NOT KNOCK UNLESS I NEED TO CALL 911." I put the sign up for thirty-minute increments, and then I would come out to hang with the kids once I was ready. If I need more time or have to take a nap, then I delegate one of the older siblings to be in charge. I then inform all the kids of who is in charge, and put my note back on my door.

This system effectively allows me to get the break I need in between any Carter Crew crises, burning dinner rolls, kid fights, and our nightly preparation schedules. I often hear my children approaching the door and say, "Oh, we have to wait because the sign is up!" Once I saw how communicative this was, I made other signs such as "Conference Call" for when I have to conduct work meetings from home. I even made a sign that states, "Mom is not available but Dad is." For many families, kids run to mama first, even when dad is home.

CHAPTER 10

INTENTIONAL

So, let's answer some basic questions: *How* do you become intentional about the words you say and why is it so important?

Growing up in a Christian home afforded me the opportunity to learn at an early age the power of positivity, having faith, and believing for what I ask. In my late teens and early adulthood, I continued the principles that I learned as a little girl but, as my obligations and my role in life became greater, I needed more support to not get swallowed up by life.

In 2008, while my youngest son had a minor procedure called a bilateral myringotomy in which a tiny tube, called the pressure equalization (PE) or tympanostomy tube, is inserted into the eardrum to ventilate and equalize pressure in the middle ear. During the procedure, he had a seizure on the operating table. It was not reoccurring and he has never had one since, but as protocol, he had to follow up with a neurologist.

Once there, the neurologist showed me the imaging scan of his brain. One side of his brain was normal, similar to a maze perfectly winding back and forth, but the other side was not of normal development. All of the separating lines throughout that side of his brain were all blended together, similar to a bowl of oatmeal. During my adopted son's pregnancy, his biological mother struggled with substance abuse; therefore, my son's brain never fully developed, a condition known as right cerebral mal-development. This was information that I knew since adoption but it was my first time seeing an image of his brain. The doctor told me to continue to watch for signs of seizures as it could present itself in many ways. Well, this peaked my curiosity about the brain.

In my research, I read details about what is known as the reticular activating system (RAS). Your RAS acts as a filter of data that your brain receives, which can be over two million pieces of information about sounds, taste, colors, picture, and images, all at any given time. The brain can only handle so much, and thus, the RAS filter what is important to you. How does it know what is important to you? It filters this information by what you concentrate on the most. As we speak and focus on situations, our brain remembers what we have spoken and focused on in the past and matches that with congruent situations.

As I begin to read about the RAS function in our brain, I realized that this is what I have been doing since I was a young adult: Focusing on exactly what I wanted. Of course, I didn't realize the science behind it; I only knew the scriptures in the Bible that would tell me to "think on these things" and "believe that you receive them" and "all my desire is before thee."

—Philippians 4:8, Finally, brethren, whatsoever things are true, whatsoever things are honest, whatsoever things are just, whatsoever things are pure, whatsoever things are lovely, whatsoever things are of good report; if there be any virtue, and if there be any praise, think on these things, or the scripture that stated "believe that you receive them.

—Mark 11:24, Therefore I say unto you, What things so ever ye desire, when ye pray, believe that ye receive them, and ye shall have them, or the scripture that stated "all my desire is before you.

—Psalm 38:9, Lord, all my desire is before thee; and my groaning is not hid from thee.

When you speak of positivity and life, you attract the same. It also works in reverse: If you are speaking negativity and defeat into situations, you attract the same. It's the same concept as when you get a new car, and the next day, you seem to notice everyone with the same car. Or when you suddenly see lots of pregnant women after you yourself get pregnant. That is how the RAS in your brain operates in your day-today.

As I stated before, I didn't understand the science behind any of this years ago—I just held true to my faith and beliefs. Others would ask how did I do certain things or get exactly what I ask for, or even question if I am telling the truth about my story, and all I could say is I prayed and believed for it. When you have found something in your life that truly works, you don't have to feel bad if others don't understand it or think it's not true.

Imagine you have a child that is allergic to a certain plant and you find a lotion that works wonders on your child's arm where the allergic reaction happens. You have been using it for years, but then, someone comes along and says, "Are you sure that works? I had another friend that tried it and it didn't work for them." Your response or thought may be something similar to, "I'm sorry it didn't work for you when you tried it but I know this works for my family and I am not going to change it now." That is how I felt about my life, and reading books and studies on the brain made me smile because what the world is still learning, as more and more studies continue, I learned directly from our maker, God.

Now, it can be tough to help your children understand the concept of being intentional about the words they say; however, when they see prayers answered or things happened that they know was talked about as a family, then they understand the bigger picture. Try it with your family. It's not always easy, but I know from experience that what you water will grow. If you make this a continual habit, your life will change and all, including your children, will see the benefits of developing and maintaining the habit of being intentional about the words they say. It is not to discount bad things that happen or act like they don't exist, but as you move forward, your continual focus is on how it will change for your good or how something beneficial will come out of it. As Romans 8:28 says, "And we know that all things work together for good to them that love God, to them who are the called according to his purpose."

As I learned more about being intentional with my words, I became intentional about my time and intentional about how I spend money. In addition, I began to prepare more: Afterall, when you prepare for what you believe in, "preparation positions you for opportunity." As a foster parent for the last fourteen years, I have cared for many children. One sibling set I had required extra TLC that I could not provide while working full time; so, I stayed home to care for a five-year-old boy and his two-year-old little sister, along with my six children. They were in my care for almost two years.

After being successfully reunited with their mother, I decided it was time for me to go back to work. With intentionality, I prepared for what I had faith in, or for what I believed, which was to go back to work after caring for our foster kids. I dry cleaned suits to wear for interviews, I prepared my resume, I got a fresh haircut, and then I started submitting my resume. Two hours after submitting about five resumes, I received a call for an interview, which was scheduled three days later, and I was hired on the spot. This is an example of the RAS matching what I believed. The vibes that I remitted called in what I sent out. As Hebrews 11:1 notes, "Now faith is the substance of things hoped for, the evidence of things not seen." And Romans 12:2: "And do not be conformed to this world, but be transformed by the renewing of your mind, that you may prove what is that good and acceptable and perfect will of God."

Here are some practical ways of being intentional about the words you speak:

❯ Pray with your children before they go to school or bed. They can lead the prayers, too.

❯ Say grace at meal times demonstrating thankfulness.

❯ Teach siblings about how to ask nicely and encourage sharing.

❯ Respond when a child asks for help, with manners. Don't respond to whining.

❯ Ask teens questions so that they can express themselves with their own words.

❯ Sit down at the dinner table with your children and teach them table manners, and talk about how well they are doing.

❯ Have your children show you how to do their homework and commend their leadership skills.

❯ Share challenging parts of the day with the whole family.

❯ Share with your children your family's mission and purpose or develop one together.

CHAPTER 11

IMAGINE

"What we think, we become."

—Buddha

As mothers, we have those days where unforeseen and unpredictable situations seem to find us all day long. Everything that could go wrong goes wrong. There are often times we don't allow ourselves moments to breathe before moving on to the next agenda item in our day. When we get home, we don't unwind or give ourselves permission for quiet time; instead, we will allow the erupting volcano to explode onto our children. In those situations, we find ourselves saying things we don't mean to say and/or with emotion that we did not intend. Because our words are so powerful a moment of agitation, can turn it into a memory of emotional turbulence.

Imagine speaking a declaration or prayer over your child and they come home to report good news, because you said so. Imagine your child speaking into existence and sharing with you the job they hope to obtain, and they receive the call for the job offer because they said so. Imagine using the power of your words to speak life to a dead relationship between an estranged son or daughter, and it changes because you said so. Imagine speaking destiny into your child's day and future, and awesome things happen because you said so. Imagine speaking to a situation where it is doubtful that any of your kids would be accepted into a program, but to everyone's amazement, all three of your children are accepted, because you said so.

Well, guess what? You don't have to imagine anymore because you have been equipped with the power of words to speak to any situation in your life. And be specific about what you want and say so! This way, when it happens, you know it's because you spoke it into existence. Have you ever imagined your ideal car or dress? You spend many days dreaming and thinking about this fantasy thing, and once you see it, you know it's the one because it's just like you imagined it to be. The same thing happens when you speak things into existence. I want this type of work environment, I want to marry this type of guy, I want to take this type of trip—we do it all the time for things unknowingly or unintentionally, but you can apply the same techniques intentionally to see change in various areas of your life, especially in the lives of our children. Just like we do with other things, we can teach our children the same technique. Start small and build from there, which will also build their confidence.

HAVE YOU HEARD SOME OF THESE PHRASES?

Oh no, it's going to be a bad day.

I woke up on the wrong side of the bed.

I always lose my keys.

I'm always late.

I'm never one time to anything.

I'm so forgetful.

It must be a Monday.

I am a failure.

I'm never going to get out of debt.

I'm never going to find true love.

I never win anything.

Good things never happen to me.

I'm having a bad day.

This is going to kill me.

I'm never going to finish this.

I suck at this.

Nobody likes me.

I do not deserve to be love.

I can't do this.

I'm such a dummy.

That is impossible.

I am not good enough.

I don't deserve that.

If we heard our children saying some of these phrases, we would quickly reiterate to them that none of it is true and that they have the power and knowledge to do anything they want. It's no different when you say these things to yourself as an adult. We have to include positivity if we want it in return. You will get a lot further with a positive mindset.

HAVE YOU HEARD SOME OF THESE PHRASES?

I always get picked.

I deserve this.

Today is going to be a great day.

I woke up ready.

I always find my keys.

I'm always on time.

I have a great memory.

It's Motivation Monday.

Failure is not an option.

I am getting out of debt.

I will find true love.

I always win.

Good things always happen to me.

This is going to be great for me.

I will finish.

I am a quick learner.

I can do it.

Where there's a will, there's a way.

Speaking with a positive mindset doesn't mean you don't acknowledge when things go wrong; it just means that you are being intentional about your words and your focus is on moving forward.

Because I said so, I will have to make what I say "so."

ABOUT THE AUTHOR

Leona Carter is an author, speaker, life coach, community advocate, and parent educator. Born and raised in Seattle, Washington, she married her high school sweetheart, Omarr, and they currently reside in Kalamazoo, Michigan, with their six children.

As a human service professional and foster parent of fourteen years, Carter has been blessed by the communities in which she has lived and currently lives, as well as the opportunities afforded to her and her family. In her spare time, she enjoys reading, writing, singing, dancing, and acting in local plays. She also enjoys challenging her husband in a game of scrabble, and he sometimes lets her win.

To connect with Leona Carter, visit her website at **facebook.com/toblikehim**

purposely created
PUBLISHING

CREATING DISTINCTIVE BOOKS
WITH INTENTIONAL RESULTS

We're a collaborative group of creative masterminds
with a mission to produce high-quality books to position
you for monumental success in the marketplace.

Our professional team of writers, editors, designers,
and marketing strategists work closely together to ensure
that every detail of your book is a clear representation
of the message in your writing.

Want to know more?
Write to us at info@publishyourgift.com
or call (888) 949-6228

Discover great books, exclusive offers, and more at
www.PublishYourGift.com

Connect with us on social media

@publishyourgift

CPSIA information can be obtained
at www.ICGtesting.com
Printed in the USA
FFOW02n0813061017
40734FF